KU-537-640

Pretty Fly for a Mai Tai

Pretty Fly for a Mai Tai

COCKTAILS
with
ROCK 'N' ROLL
SPIRIT

illustrations by Ben Tallon

MITCHELL BEAZLEY

Contents

Interlude

Appetite for Destruction
Shots & Shooters

91

Side B

The Kids Are Alright
The Modern Age

101

Introduction

Rock'n'roll, noun

'A category of popular music centred largely on guitar, bass, drums and vocals... Popularized in the 1950s, and usually incorporating tuneful melodies, simple chord structures and a heavy, rhythmic beat.'

That right there is the dictionary definition of rock 'n' roll, although there is an alternative school of thought on the subject, peddled by sweaty Aussie rockers AC/DC on their 1977 anthem *Let There Be Rock*. In it, they claim rock 'n' roll was in fact invented by the great Russian composer Tchaikovsky. Like some mad alchemist, he cried: 'Let there be sound!' and there was sound. 'Let there be light!' he cried. And there was light. 'Let there be drums! And there were drums. And so on and so forth, until finally, he'd invented the greatest of all music genres.

The 1950s theory begs to differ, arguing that rock 'n' roll was born when the influences of boogie woogie, jazz, gospel and blues had it away with an electric guitar. Elvis Presley made it popular, sold it to the masses and the rest, as historians are fond of saying, is history.

Whatever the truth, what we can all agree on is that rock 'n' roll music is clearly a mix of various influences. Therefore it is the very definition of a cocktail. But here's another one...

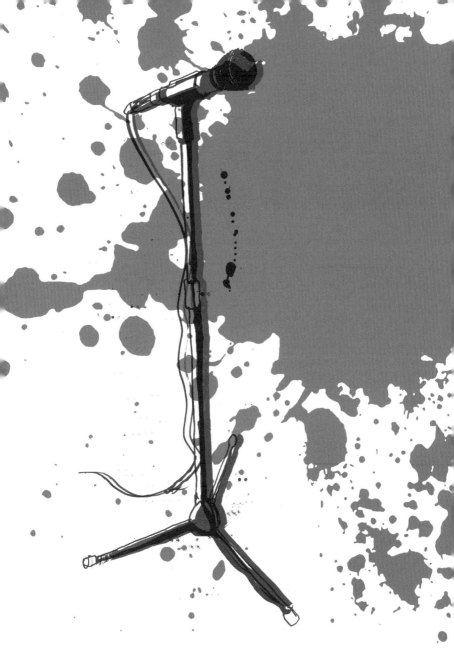

Cocktail, noun

'A blend of an alcoholic spirit or several spirits and other ingredients; for example, fruit juice, cola or cream'

The history of the cocktail goes back much further than the birth of rock 'n' roll. As far back as 1806, a New York publication entitled *The Balance and Columbian Repository* ran a question asking 'What is a cocktail?' Its editor replied that a cocktail 'is a stimulating liquor, composed of spirits of any kind, sugar, water and bitters – it is vulgarly called bittered sling'. He added that once under the influence of this revolutionary new tipple, drinkers became fuddle-headed and easily led. Even so, this most liberating libation quickly caught on and the rest, as cocktail historians will tell you, is cocktail history.

But the story doesn't end there. Later, much later, there followed a quite ingenious twist. Inspired by the fact that rock stars and alcohol have always enjoyed a symbiotic relationship, someone clever took the two elements and mixed them together. Rock 'n' roll + cocktails, shaken and stirred = The Rocktail.

The Rocktail, noun

'A rock-based cocktail, guzzled while listening to classic rock, lightly banging one's head, probably making the devil-horn hand sign and generally exhibiting the spirit of rock 'n' roll excess.'

And that's what we have right here, in the book you hold before you. Contained within its pages are 75 of the greatest rock 'n' roll-inspired cocktails ever created. Their coming together is the obvious evolution of booze and rock, made one louder and turned right up to 11. So, for those about to rock – via the medium of a nice cocktail – we most definitely salute you.

The Basics

———

Before you plough straight into the rocking,
rolling and general festivities, it's worth
familiarizing yourself with some of the tools of the
trade, and the techniques you'll need to make the
most of the recipes in this book. Come on, it's not
that hard – if Slash can learn that seven-minute
guitar solo then you can learn how to make a
citrus twist. And, if that wasn't inspiration
enough, everything here will vastly improve your
cocktail-making (and -drinking) enjoyment!

———

What is a Cocktail?

The word 'cocktail' conjures up all sorts of images, mainly associated with celebrations, entertaining and enjoyment – particularly ones involving fine company and music turned up way too loud. A cocktail is essentially a mixed drink with a spirit base (usually gin, vodka, whisky, rum or tequila) that is combined with tonic, juice or another non-alcoholic mixer. Often a third ingredient is added, a flavouring to complement the spirit and add a distinctive flavour. This can be anything from a sugar cube to Angostura bitters.

From Humble Beginnings

There are several theories about the origins of the cocktail, some more credible than others. It has been suggested that the name was adapted from the French word *coquetier*, meaning egg cup, in which the first cocktail – the Sazerac (see a Rage Against the Machine-inspired twist on page 120) – was originally served. It has also been said that the word came from a tavern in New York where the innkeeper's daughter made a drink for her intended on his return from a sailing expedition. He brought back a fighting cockerel, and the daughter used its tail feathers to decorate his drink. But many think that the cocktail came into being in the United States in the 1920s, during Prohibition. The banning of alcohol forced people to seek out interesting ways of flavouring the infamous bathtub gin and other bootleg liquors, giving the cocktail authentic lo-fi, homemade – some might even say punk – origins.

Choosing Glasses

There are thousands of different cocktails, but they all fall into one of three categories: long, short or shot. Long drinks generally have more mixer than alcohol and are often served with ice and a straw. The terms 'straight up' and 'on the rocks' are synonymous with the short drink, which tends to be more about the spirit, which is often combined with a single mixer, at most. Finally, there is the shot. These miniature cocktails are made up mainly from spirits and liqueurs and are designed to give a quick hit of alcohol. Cocktail glasses are tailored to the types of drinks they will contain.

WINE GLASS
Sangria (see page 132) is often served in a wine glass, but they are not usually used for cocktails.

MARTINI GLASS
A martini glass, also known as a cocktail glass, is designed so that your hand can't warm the glass, making sure that the cocktail is served completely chilled.

MARGARITA OR COUPETTE GLASS
When this type of glass is used for a margarita, the rim is dipped in salt. These glasses can be used for daiquiris and other fruit-based cocktails.

HIGHBALL GLASS
A highball glass is suitable for any long cocktail, such as the Everlong Island Iced Tea (see page 130).

CHAMPAGNE FLUTE
Used for Champagne or Champagne cocktails, the narrow mouth of the flute helps the drink to stay fizzy.

CHAMPAGNE SAUCER
These old-fashioned glasses are not very practical for serving Champagne because the drink quickly loses its fizz.

OLD-FASHIONED GLASS
Also known as a rocks glass, the old-fashioned glass is great for any drink that's served on the rocks or straight up. It's also good for muddled drinks.

SHOT GLASS
Shot glasses are often found in two sizes — for a single or double measure. They are ideal for a single mouthful.

BALLOON GLASS
These glasses are usually used for fine spirits, where aroma is as important as the taste. The glass can be warmed to encourage the release of the aroma.

HURRICANE GLASS
This type of glass is mostly found in beach bars, where it is used to serve creamy, rum-based drinks.

BOSTON GLASS
Often used by bartenders for mixing cocktails, the Boston glass is also good for fruity drinks.

TODDY GLASS
A toddy glass is generally used for a hot drink, such as an Irish Coffee. See page 149 for a hot cocktail worthy of a king (of Leon).

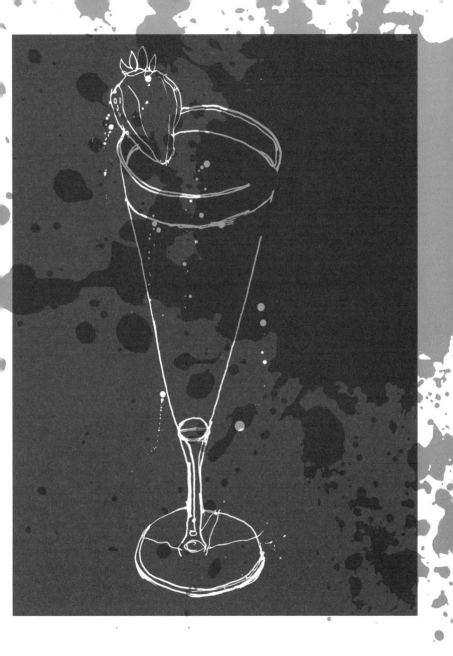

Useful Equipment

The only truly essential equipment when it comes to making the recipes in this book are the ingredients, the will and a non-stop soundtrack of the finest songs rock 'n' roll has to offer. Having said that, there are a few tools that are worth investing in if you want to make the very most of the drinks on offer.

SHAKER
The Boston shaker is the simplest option, but it needs to be used in conjunction with a Hawthorne strainer (see below). Alternatively, you could choose a shaker with a built-in strainer.

MIXING GLASS
A mixing glass is used for those drinks that require only a gentle stirring before they are poured or strained.

FOOD PROCESSOR
A food processor or blender is useful for making frozen cocktails and smoothies.

HAWTHORNE STRAINER
This type of strainer is often used in conjunction with a Boston shaker, but a tea strainer will also work well.

MUDDLING STICK
Similar to a pestle, which will work just as well, a muddling stick, or muddler, is used to crush fruit or herbs in a glass or shaker for drinks like a mojito.

BAR SPOON
Similar to a teaspoon but with a long handle, a bar spoon is used for stirring, layering and muddling drinks.

MEASURE OR JIGGER
Single and double measures are available and are essential when you are mixing ingredients so that the proportions are always the same. One measure is 25ml or 1 fl oz.

BOTTLE OPENER
One of the more essential items, some bottle openers have two attachments: one for metal-topped bottles and a corkscrew for wine bottles.

POURERS
A pourer is inserted into the top of a spirit bottle to enable the spirit to flow in a controlled manner.

The Spirits and their Partners

Each spirit has a natural affinity with certain flavours, and it is from these complementary relationships that cocktails are born. All spirits, of course, have a natural affinity with the spirit of rock 'n' roll.

BRANDY
Much brandy is distilled from grapes, but there are some varieties that use other fruits as their base. Serve brandy with fruit and fruit juices, but don't use the finest brandies for mixed drinks.

GIN
A clear grain spirit infused with juniper berries, gin was first produced in Holland over 400 years ago. Serve it with citrus fruits, fresh berries and tonic water.

RUM
This Caribbean staple, which dates back to the 17th century, is made from sugar cane left over after sugar production. Serve rum with any of the exotic fruits, cream or cola.

TEQUILA
Mexico's best-known spirit is made from the blue agave plant, and its origins can be traced back to the Aztecs. It was traditionally served by itself as a tequila slammer, but also works well with citrus and sour fruits as well as ginger and tomato.

VODKA

Vodka is distilled from grain and is relatively free from natural flavour. There is a fierce debate as to its origins, with both the Poles and the Russians claiming to have invented the drink. With its neutral character, it is infinitely mixable with a huge range of flavours. Serve it with cranberry, tomato or citrus juices – or for a classic drink, simply add tonic water.

WHISKY

The origins of whisky are hotly debated, with both Scotland and Ireland staking a claim to have developed it. Modern whiskies have a much smoother taste and texture, and there are two main types: blended and unblended. Serve it with water, soda water, cola or ginger ale.

SUGAR SYRUP

This is used as a sweetener in lots of cocktails. It blends into a cold drink more quickly than sugar and adds body. You can buy this in bottles, but it's very easy to make your own. Simply bring equal quantities of caster sugar and water to the boil in a small saucepan, stirring continuously, then boil for 1–2 minutes without stirring. Sugar syrup can be kept in a sterilized bottle in the refrigerator for up to 2 months.

Perfecting Your Technique

Your bartending will vastly improve with a few simple techniques

---

BLENDING

Frozen cocktails and smoothies are blended with ice into a smooth consistency.
A frozen daiquiri or margarita uses a virtually identical recipe to the unfrozen
version but with a scoop of crushed ice added before blending on high speed.
Don't add too much ice as this will dilute the cocktail; just add a little at a time.

MUDDLING

Muddling is a technique that is used to bring out the flavours of herbs and fruit
using a blunt tool called a muddler. The best-known muddled drink is the mojito
(see page 104 for a Clash-inspired take on this classic).

1. Add mint leaves, sugar syrup and lime wedges to a highball glass.
2. Hold the glass firmly and use a muddler or pestle to press down.
Twist and press to release the flavours.
3. Continue this for about 30 seconds, then top up the glass
with crushed ice and add the remaining ingredients.

SHAKING

The best-known cocktail technique and probably the one that you use most
often, so it's important to get right. Shaking is used to mix ingredients quickly
and thoroughly, and to chill the drink before serving.

1. Half-fill a cocktail shaker with ice cubes, or cracked or crushed ice.
2. If the recipe calls for a chilled glass add a few ice cubes and
some cold water to the glass, swirl it around and discard.
3. Add the recipe ingredients to the shaker and shake until a frost forms on the
outside. Use both hands, one at each end, so that it doesn't slip.
4. Strain the cocktail into the glass and serve.

BUILDING

This straightforward technique involves nothing more than putting the ingredients together in the correct order.

1. Have all the ingredients for the cocktail to hand. Chill the glass, if required.
2. Add each ingredient in recipe order, making sure that all measures are exact.

DOUBLE-STRAINING

When you want to prevent all traces of puréed fruit and ice fragments from entering the glass, use a shaker with a built-in strainer in conjunction with a Hawthorne strainer. Alternatively, strain through a fine strainer.

LAYERING

A number of spirits can be served layered on top of each other, and because some spirits are lighter than others, they will float on top of your cocktail.

1. Pour the first ingredient into a glass, taking care that it does not touch the sides.
2. Position a bar spoon in the centre of the glass, rounded part down and facing you. Rest the spoon against the side of the glass as your pour the second ingredient down the spoon. It should float on top of the first liquid, creating a separate layer.
3. Repeat with the third ingredient, then carefully remove the spoon.

STIRRING

A cocktail is prepared by stirring when the ingredients need to be mixed and chilled, but it's important to maintain the clarity. This ensures that there is no fragmented ice or air bubbles throughout the drink. Some stirred cocktails will require the ingredients to be prepared in a mixing glass, then strained into the serving glass with a fine strainer.

1. Add the ingredients to a glass in the order stated in the recipe.
2. Use a bar spoon to stir the drink, lightly or vigorously, as described in the recipe.
3. Finish the drink with any decoration and serve.

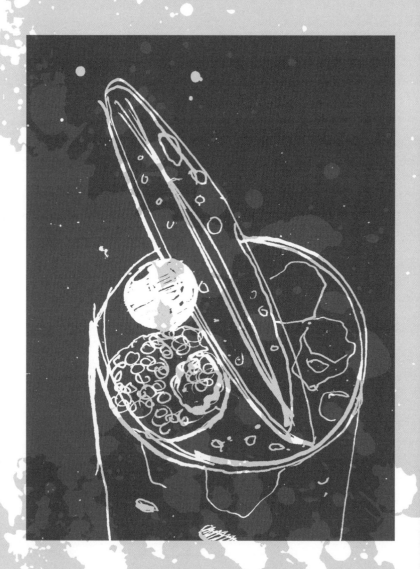

The Finishing Touches

Some cocktails are decorated for decoration's sake, but in others the decoration is a vital part of the flavour — the green olive in a dry martini, for example. Decorations can range from a simple twist of lemon to a complicated assemblage of fruit on a cocktail stick. The possibilities are almost endless, ranging from celery sticks, slices of cucumber, cracked pepper and cherry tomatoes to prawns and even quails' eggs (though the latter suggestions are perhaps best suited to cocktails that accompany some of the more flamboyant songs in this book).

WEDGES

Citrus fruits work well as wedges. The wedge can be squeezed into the drink, then dropped in or served on the rim of the glass. Simply slide a sharp knife through the flesh so that you can balance it on the rim.

SLICES AND WHEELS

Any round fruit, such as kiwi fruit, limes, lemons, oranges and apples, can be cut into cross-sections to create wheels or slices (half-wheels). You can either place the wheel or slice on the rim of the glass or float it on the surface of the drink. Use your imagination and take your inspiration from the flavours in the cocktail.

TWISTS

Citrus twists not only look good but also impart flavour to the cocktail. Pare a strip of rind from the fruit and remove all signs of pith. Twist the rind over the surface of the drink to release the oils, then drop it into the drink. Flaming the rind before twisting it releases even more flavour.

SPIRALS

Citrus spirals look great when they are draped over the side of the drink or dropped into it. Use a cannelle knife to cut a long, thin strip of rind from the fruit. and wind it around a cylinder, such as a bar spoon, straw or swizzle stick, to create a spiral. Hold it for a few seconds to allow it to set into shape.

FRUIT KEBABS

Miniature kebabs can be balanced on top of drinks or placed in them. Try a combination of berries in descending order of size, such as a strawberry, blackberry, raspberry and blueberry, or use fruit of matching colours. Another option is to pick out fruits that feature in the flavouring of the cocktail. Simply thread them onto a cocktail stick.

HERBS

Sprigs of herbs make attractive and fragrant decorations. They can be used to decorate the glass or be placed in the drink.

NOVELTY DECORATIONS

Some novelty decorations are not as popular as they once were, but can still look great with the right cocktail – something about a paper umbrella, for example, calls to mind the excess of 1980s hair metal. Paper umbrellas, plastic monkeys and even sparklers are just a few of the options available to liven up your drinks.

FROSTING

Although it is not strictly a decoration, frosting a glass does add a very professional finishing touch to a drink. Frosting can add flavour, as in the salt used for the margarita (see page 63 for a Springsteen-inspired twist), or it can be just visual, as with some sugar frostings. To add a frosting, dip the rim of the glass in a saucer of lime or lemon juice or water. Spread the sugar or salt on a small plate and place the rim of the glass in the frosting. Twist to give an even coating and use a lime or lemon wedge to clean off any excess frosting from inside of the glass to prevent it from contaminating the cocktail. If you want to be sure that the frosting will stay in place, use egg white in place of the citrus juice to stick the sugar or salt to the glass.

Old Time Rock 'n' Roll

THE CLASSICS

*

What constitutes a 'classic' rock track? We pondered this question long and hard, scratching our heads, stroking our beards and generally pontificating for what seemed like a lifetime. We finally answered it by compiling a long list of what we consider to be true classics of the rock canon. Now you may not agree with every last one of our selections here – 'Where's "Hocus Pocus" by Focus?' you may cry – but we're confident that every cut on Side A stands up as a stone-cold classic.

Our 37 tracks span a 22-year period and take us on a musical journey that begins in 1957 and ends in 1979, from Elvis Presley's prison cell down into the stomach of Pink Floyd's Roger Waters – via a crack house in Harlem, the Highway to Hell and a mythical hotel that you can never leave.

En route we'll encounter a cast of many, including the devil incarnate. We'll learn the true identity of Jumpin' Jack Flash and even discover why a batch of lumpy mashed potato inspired one of Jimi Hendrix's finest tracks.

But wait! 'What constitutes a 'classic' rock cocktail?' you might also ask.

Well, turn the page and you'll soon find out, because we've complemented each classic track with its own classic cocktail. So, as the great Marty DiBergi once said, enough of my yakkin'. Let's rock!

Jailhouse on the Rocks

JAILHOUSE ROCK
ELVIS PRESLEY
1957

More noted in latter years for his gluttony than for any real appreciation of cocktails, Elvis Presley would still find much to admire in our Jailhouse on the Rocks. It's a classic mix of vodka, Amaretto di Saronno and ice that's gently stirred rather than, ahem, all shook up. Inspired by The King's 1957 cut 'Jailhouse Rock', in which our lip-quivering hero attends a party in the county jail, it's a safe bet they weren't drinking any of this in the can. Serve with deep-fried peanut butter vol-au-vents for the full Elvis effect.

MAKES 2

cracked ice cubes

3 measures vodka

1 measure Amaretto di Saronno

METHOD

Put 4–6 cracked ice cubes into 2 old-fashioned glasses. Add the vodka and Amaretto di Saronno, stir lightly to mix and serve.

Like an Aperol-ing Stone

LIKE A ROLLING STONE
BOB DYLAN
1965

Ah, we've all been there, on our own, no direction home; lost and lonely after a night on the booze, embarking on a wobbly-legged walk in the vague direction of home. Given his penchant for heavy politics back in '65, maybe that's not what Dylan had in mind with this one but, even so, in honour of this masterpiece that weighs in at a then-unheard-of six-plus minutes long, may we present Like An Aperol-ing Stone – a classic mix of Aperol, grapefruit and soda water. Oh, and may we suggest you take a cab home afterwards.

✻

MAKES 1

1 measure Aperol

2 measures grapefruit juice

4 measures soda water

ice cubes

grapefruit wedge, to decorate

METHOD

Add the Aperol, grapefruit juice and soda water to a wine glass full of ice cubes. Stir, decorate with a grapefruit wedge and serve.

Subterranean Homesick
Blue Hawaii

SUBTERRANEAN HOMESICK BLUES
BOB DYLAN
1965

Yes, it's the one with the video in which a black-and-white Dylan shuffles prompt boards containing scrawled lyrics. Bob sang in a verbal whirlwind about someone called Johnny mixing up medicine while he himself was outside, thinking about the government. Whoever Johnny was, he should have been mixing up a Subterranean Homesick Blue Hawaii instead; it would have lifted his symptoms quicker than any medicine. Pour one for Bob too, Johnny, and take his mind off politics, if only for a little while.

✳

MAKES 1

1 scoop crushed ice

1 measure white rum

½ measure blue Curaçao

2 measures pineapple juice

1 measure coconut cream

pineapple wedge, to decorate

METHOD

Put the crushed ice into a blender. Add the remaining ingredients and blend on high speed for 20–30 seconds. Pour into a chilled martini glass. Decorate with a pineapple wedge and serve.

My Gin-eration

✣

MY GENERATION
THE WHO
1965

If ever there was a song that encapsulated the angst of being a spotty, snotty teenager during the Swinging Sixties, it would be this. 'My Generation' remains a timeless nod to Mod counterculture, a forebear to the punk rock movement, an angry, anthemic tirade, all delivered with that famous stutter by Roger Daltrey. You don't have to be on speed to summon the punk spirit here, though.

Just whip up a My Gin-eration and relax and gently f-f-f-fade away.

✣

MAKES 2

8 raspberries, plus extra to decorate

8 blueberries, plus extra to decorate

1–2 dashes strawberry syrup

crushed ice

4 measures gin

4 teaspoons lemon juice

sugar syrup, to taste

soda water, to top up

lemon slices, to decorate

METHOD

Muddle half the berries and strawberry syrup in the bottom of each highball glass, then fill each glass with crushed ice. Add half the gin, lemon juice and sugar syrup to each glass. Stir well, then top up with soda water. Decorate with raspberries, blueberries and a lemon slice.

Dedicated Follower of Old-Fashioned

DEDICATED FOLLOWER OF FASHION
THE KINKS
1966

In the glorious, swinging London of the Sixties, Kinks songwriter and lead vocalist Ray Davies attended a soirée and found himself arguing with a designer over the futility of fashion. The argument quickly turned physical and they were soon trading blows, with Davies later admitting to lashing out a kick or two. Now obviously we cannot condone such behaviour, but on such moments of mindless brawling does rock 'n' roll history change. That kick inspired this classic track, which in turn inspired this classic cocktail. And we'll all drink to that.

✳

MAKES 1

ice cubes

2 measures bourbon

1 teaspoon sugar syrup

1 dash orange bitters

1 dash Angostura bitters

orange wheel, to decorate

METHOD

Half-fill an old-fashioned glass with ice cubes. Add the remaining ingredients to the glass and stir for 1 minute. Fill the glass with more ice cubes. Decorate with an orange wheel and serve.

I'm Waiting for the Mango

I'M WAITING FOR THE MAN
VELVET UNDERGROUND
1967

According to the fascinating lyrics, 'The Man' was a Harlem drug dealer who peddled his wares close to the intersection of New York's Lexington Avenue and 125th Street. The man waiting for 'The Man' was an incongruous white cat looking to purchase $26 worth of heroin. Later, having completed the transaction, cooked up his drugs and pumped them into his body, he complains of feeling more dead than alive. Some advice for the man, then: next time, simply whip up this cocktail instead. It contains mango, which helps bump up your daily intake of healthy fruits. Heroin doesn't – at least not last time we checked.

✳

MAKES 2

crushed ice

1 ripe mango, peeled and stoned, plus extra slices to decorate

6 coconut chunks

2 measures coconut cream

4 measures aged rum

2 dashes lemon juice

2 teaspoons caster sugar

METHOD

Put a small scoop of crushed ice with all the other ingredients into a food processor or blender and blend until smooth. Transfer to 2 hurricane glasses, decorate with mango slices and serve with long straws.

The Wind Cries Bloody Mary

THE WIND CRIES MARY
JIMI HENDRIX
1967

'The Wind Cries Mary' was allegedly written after Jimi Hendrix and his then-girlfriend argued over her inability to make lump-free mashed potato. Kathy Etchingham wasn't much of a cook but she was better than Hendrix, whose talents lay more in psychedelic blues. So when he complained about her lumpy mash, she threw some plates and stormed out. Hendrix grabbed his axe and cooked up one of rock's greatest ballads, using Etchingham's middle name, Mary, to wind her up further. So, in honour, raise a glass of The Wind Cries Bloody Mary to Kathy. She makes terrible mash but an awesome cocktail.

❋

MAKES 1

ice cubes

2 measures vodka

1 dash fresh lemon juice

Worcestershire sauce, to taste

tomato juice, to top up

½ teaspoon cayenne pepper

salt and pepper

celery stalks, to decorate

cherry tomato, to decorate

METHOD

Put some ice cubes into a highball glass. Pour over the vodka and lemon juice, add Worcestershire sauce to taste and top up with tomato juice. Add the cayenne pepper and season to taste with salt and pepper. Stir to chill. Decorate with celery stalks and a cherry tomato and serve.

Waterloo Sunrise

WATERLOO SUNSET
THE KINKS
1967

Though believed by most to be an ode to the London skyline, in recent years chief Kink Ray Davies has suggested 'Waterloo Sunset' was actually inspired by the suburb of Waterloo in Liverpool, on the banks of the dirty old River Mersey, looking out across the Irish S... What's that? You don't care either way, you just want some booze? Ah yes, okay. Some booze. Well, how about a Waterloo Sunrise, a clever titular twist inspired by the classic Tequila Sunrise. As long as you gaze on a Waterloo Sunrise, as Ray Davies (almost) sang, you'll be in paradise.

✢

MAKES 2

5–6 ice cubes

3 measures tequila

200 ml (7 fl oz) fresh orange juice

4 teaspoons grenadine

orange slices, to decorate

METHOD

Put the ice cubes in a cocktail shaker, add the tequila and fresh orange juice. Shake to mix. Strain into 2 highball glasses over plenty of ice, then slowly pour 2 teaspoons of grenadine into each one, allowing it to settle. Decorate each glass with an orange slice.

Sgt. Pepper's Lonely Hearts Club Brandy

SGT. PEPPER'S LONELY HEARTS CLUB BAND
THE BEATLES
1967

The Beatles' eighth album is considered by many to be the soundtrack to the 'Summer of Love', and one of the most inventive and influential albums ever created. You'll know it best as the album with the cover featuring the four of them surrounded by a collage of characters they admired. But that was no a collage; it actually happened. All the people pictured had gathered in the studio at Abbey Road for a cocktail party in which the band unveiled its latest mix; the Sgt. Pepper's Lonely Hearts Club Brandy. It kicked like a mule and got the double thumbs-up from Macca.

✻

MAKES 2

lemon wedges

caster sugar

4 measures brandy

1 measure orange Curaçao

1 measure maraschino liqueur

2 measures lemon juice

6 dashes Angostura bitters

ice cubes

lemon rind strips, to decorate

METHOD

Moisten the rim of 2 chilled martini glasses with a lemon wedge, then dip them in the caster sugar. Put the brandy, Curaçao, maraschino, lemon juice and bitters into a cocktail shaker with some ice cubes and shake well. Strain into the glasses, decorate each with lemon rind strips and serve.

A Rusty Shade of Nail

A WHITER SHADE OF PALE
PROCOL HARUM
1967

Procol Harum's Hammond-powered hit told of skipping the light fandango and turning cartwheels as the ceiling blew off, in the midst of which a dutiful waiter appears with a tray a drinks. And on that tray, we do so pray, sat a round of Rusty Shade of Nails, inspired by a song that supposedly told of a drunken sexual escapade gone wrong. Drunken sexual escapades often follow a night on 'The Nail' – as do light fandangos and ill-advised cartwheels, incidentally.

MAKES 2

ice cubes

3 measures Scotch whisky

2 measures Drambuie

METHOD

Fill 2 old-fashioned glasses with ice cubes.
Pour over half the whisky and Drambuie
into each glass and serve.

Bourbon to Be Wild

BORN TO BE WILD
STEPPENWOLF
1968

A throbbing, turbo-charged, heavy-riffing rock classic, Steppenwolf's 'Born to Be Wild' remains as relevant today as it was in the raucous, revolting Sixties that spawned it. Frontman John Kay reflected that every generation thinks that it, too, is born wild – and can identify with the song by dancing round and making motorbike noises while mixing up cocktails based loosely on the title of the track. Okay, so he didn't really say that second part, but we're fairly certain that's what he meant. And for those occasions, this cocktail right here is your go-to guy...

﹡

MAKES 1

ice cubes

2 measures bourbon

3 teaspoons orange liqueur

2 teaspoons lemon juice

4 measures ginger beer

2 dashes Angostura bitters

METHOD

Fill a Collins glass with ice cubes, add the remaining ingredients and stir.

Gin Fizzy for the Devil

SYMPATHY FOR THE DEVIL
THE ROLLING STONES
1968

This seminal Stones number details many of the Devil's darkest dealings, set to a samba beat and with all the grunts, whoops and oinks we've come to expect from Michael P. Jagger. If the song was a cocktail, we'd venture it would be a frisky mix of gin, agave syrup, hibiscus tea, pink grapefruit juice, sparkling wine and raspberries. Woo hoo, indeed.

MAKES 4

- 1½ measures agave syrup
- 4 measures gin
- ice cubes
- 250 ml (8 fl oz) hibiscus tea
- 4 measures pink grapefruit juice
- 250 ml (8 fl oz) sparkling wine
- raspberries, to decorate

METHOD

Add the agave syrup and gin to a large jug and stir until the syrup dissolves. Fill the jug with ice cubes and add the hibiscus tea, pink grapefruit juice and sparkling wine and stir. Decorate with raspberries and serve.

All Along the Scotchtower

ALL ALONG THE WATCHTOWER
JIMI HENDRIX
1968

We could, of course, have gone for Bob Dylan's version of what we're pompously calling 'Watchtower', what with it being the original and arguably the best. But we haven't, and with good reason. If you were hosting a cocktail party and drawing up a guest list, would you rather invite grumpy Bob or psychedelic sex god Jimi Hendrix? Exactly. Hand Hendrix one of these magnificent All Along the Scotchtower cocktails and just watch him go! Oh, hold on: legend has it that Hendrix used to mix beer and red wine in a pint glass. That's pretty uncouth. Let's invite Bob round instead.

✳

MAKES 1

ice cubes

2 measures Scotch whisky

1 measure lemon juice

3 teaspoons sugar syrup

4 measures ginger ale

slice fresh root ginger, to decorate

METHOD

Pour the whisky, lemon juice, sugar syrup and ginger ale into a Collins glass filled with ice cubes and stir. Decorate with a slice of root ginger and serve.

Good Limes Bad Limes

GOOD TIMES BAD TIMES
LED ZEPPELIN
1969

That title up top may slightly mislead. When mixing up a Good Limes Bad Limes you should never ever use a bad lime. Juicy, pert, fresh little limes are as essential to this cocktail as the guitar riffs were to Led Zep, particularly on this, their anthemic debut single. Robert Plant sings of not caring what the neighbours say – a statement of intent that we cannot endorse. If the neighbours complain that your cocktail-fuelled revelry is too loud, turn the music down. Better still, mix up another round of Good Limes Bad Limes and invite them over.

*

MAKES 2

2 limes, thickly sliced

2 tablespoons thick honey

2 teaspoons caster sugar

crushed ice

4 measures vodka

METHOD

Divide the lime slices, honey and sugar into 2 heavy-based old-fashioned glasses and muddle together. Add some crushed ice and pour half the vodka into each.

Jumpin' Jack Splash

JUMPIN' JACK FLASH
THE ROLLING STONES
1970

Jumpin' Jack Flash was the gardener at 'Keef' Richards' country estate, or so the story goes. Green of fingers and fleet of foot, his work inspired Mick Jagger to write this track, in which we learn that Jack was born in a cross-fire hurricane and raised by a toothless, bearded hag. Artistic licence was possibly at work there, not to mention perhaps some mind-wobbling recreational drugs. Nonetheless, a classic track deserves a classic cocktail, and the Jumpin' Jack Splash fits the bill. To misquote Jagger himself, the 'Jumpin' Jack Splash is a gas, gas, gas!' Actually, it's a liquid, but we take his point.

❋

MAKES 2

12 mint leaves, plus sprigs to decorate

6 peach slices

6 lemon slices, plus extra to decorate

4 teaspoons caster sugar

4 measures (Jack Daniel's)

ice cubes, plus crushed ice to serve

METHOD

Muddle the mint leaves, peach and lemon slices and sugar in a cocktail shaker. Add the bourbon and some ice cubes and shake well. Strain over cracked ice into 2 old-fashioned glasses. Decorate each with a mint sprig and a lemon slice.

Won't Get Moscow Muled Again

WON'T GET FOOLED AGAIN
THE WHO
1971

Weighing in at a glorious eight-and-a-half-minutes, 'Won't Get Fooled Again' was written not as the anthem many took it to be, but as a cautionary warning on the dangers of, like, revolution, man. The track garnered critical acclaim for the way it mixed rock with what, back then, were pioneering synthesizer sounds. Our take on it is the Won't Get Moscow Muled Again, a cocktail that has garnered critical acclaim for the way it mixes vodka, fresh limes and a dash of ginger beer. Don't get fooled by its sweet, sweet taste, however. It kicks like a mule.

✣

MAKES 2

6–8 cracked ice cubes

4 measures vodka

juice of 4 limes

ginger beer, to top up

METHOD

Put the ice cubes in a cocktail shaker, add the vodka and lime juice and shake well. Pour, without straining, into 2 highball glasses over ice and top up with ginger beer.

Riders on the Dark 'n' Stormy

✻

RIDERS ON THE STORM
THE DOORS
1971

The Doors' charismatic, but perhaps slightly confused, frontman Jim Morrison wrote in a 1968 poem that he was the Lizard Kind and could do anything. This wasn't entirely true, yet one thing he definitely could have done was knock up a round of Riders on the Dark 'n' Stormy. After all, most people could – this is a very simple but very refreshing mix of dark rum, ginger beer, ice and limes.

✻

MAKES 2

ice cubes

4 measures dark rum

2 lime wedges

ginger beer, to top up

METHOD

Fill 2 highball glasses with ice cubes. Pour half the dark rum into each glass, add the lime wedges and stir. Top up with ginger beer.

Sour to the People

POWER TO THE PEOPLE
JOHN LENNON
1971

Another blast of fist-clenching, beard-stroking political activism from the solo Beatle and the Plastic Ono Band, but it's true to say 'Power to the People' wasn't John Lennon's finest hour. The hand claps were borrowed from Macca, the saxophone backing track from the *Benny Hill* theme tune and the lyrical content straight from *A Beginner's Guide to Communist Sloganeering*. Lennon himself would later admit to being slightly embarrassed by the track. Indeed, some say the best thing about the song is the whisky-fuelled cocktail it inspired. Sour to the People? Right on.

*

MAKES 1

ice cubes

2 measures Scotch whisky

1 measure lemon juice

1 measure sugar syrup

lemon wedge, to decorate

METHOD

Fill a cocktail shaker with ice cubes. Add the remaining ingredients and shake. Strain into a glass filled with ice cubes, decorate with a lemon wedge and serve.

The Gin Genie

THE JEAN GENIE

DAVID BOWIE

1973

Ah, if only there really were a Gin Genie: some magical little spirit who popped out of an empty booze bottle to grant us wishes. Imagine if he looked like a tiny version of Bowie himself in his Ziggy Stardust phase. Out in a puff of smoke he'd come, dishing out his wishes. We'd ask for a round of Gin Genies – a classic gin cream soda-style affair named after his classic track. Sadly, you can rub that bottle all you like but he won't ever appear. You're probably better off just following the instructions below.

MAKES 1

ice cubes

2 measures gin

2 teaspoons lemon juice

4 measures cream soda

black cherry and lemon wedge, to decorate

METHOD

Pour all the ingredients into a Collins glass full of ice cubes and stir. Decorate with a cherry and a lemon wedge and serve.

Tubular Bellinis

TUBULAR BELLS
MIKE OLDFIELD
1973

The first album Richard Branson's then-unknown Virgin Records ever released was an unlikely affair. A sprawling instrumental odyssey created by a teenager in his mother's loft, 'Tubular Bells' launched both Oldfield and Branson to fame and fortune. It also, inevitably, inspired several follow-ups, including 'Tubular Bells II' and 'Tubular Bells [erm] III'. Like the song, Tubular Bellinis are rather moreish, but be warned that the first round is always the easiest. Tubular Bellinis II, the difficult second cocktail, may divide opinion. It's good, no question – but is it as good as the original?

*

MAKES 2

4 measures peach juice

8 measures chilled Champagne

2 dashes grenadine (optional)

peach wedges, to decorate

METHOD

Mix together the peach juice and chilled Champagne in a large mixing glass. Add the grenadine (if used). Pour into 2 Champagne flutes, decorate each glass with a peach wedge and serve.

Margarita (Come Out Tonight)

ROSALITA (COME OUT TONIGHT)
BRUCE SPRINGSTEEN
1973

In what was apparently a true story, Rosalita's father disapproved of Bruce Springsteen chasing his daughter's affections, so he never let her out at night. Like some Seventies Romeo, The Boss sang up at her, telling her about the huge advance that the record company had just endowed him with. But Rosie's old man was having none of it and the romance fizzled out. Which is sad, but at least we can raise a glass to love's lost couple by mixing up a margarita. And unlike Rosalita, she'll always come out at night.

✳

MAKES 2

2 lime wedges

rock salt

4 measures Herradura Reposado tequila

2 measures lime juice

2 measures triple sec

ice cubes

lime slices, to decorate

METHOD

Rub the rim of 2 margarita glasses with a lime wedge, then dip each glass into rock salt. Pour the tequila, lime juice and triple sec into a cocktail shaker and add some ice cubes. Shake and strain into the salt-rimmed glasses. Decorate each glass with a slice of lime and serve.

Hotel Caipirinha

HOTEL CALIFORNIA
THE EAGLES
1977

Far superior to pink Champagne, and more readily available than the wine they stopped serving back in 1969, the Hotel Caipirinha takes the Eagles' signature cut and mixes it with Brazil's greatest – and most unpronounceable – cocktail, the Caiper... the Caipiran... ah, it's actually pronounced *cai-pir-in-ya*. The mythical 'Hotel California' was an allegory on hedonism and The American Dream turned sour. There's nothing sour about this sugary classic, which mixes cachaça, sugar, lime and ice to sweet and potent effect. It can make your head grow heavy and your sight grow dim, so moderation is the key.

✱

MAKES 2

8 lime wedges, plus extra to decorate

1 teaspoon of cane sugar

crushed ice

4 measures of cachaça

METHOD

Divide and muddle the lime wedges into 2 old-fashioned glasses with the cane sugar. Top with crushed ice and pour half the cachaça into each. Decorate with lime wedges and serve.

Negroni Rock 'n' Roll (But I Like It)

IT'S ONLY ROCK 'N' ROLL (BUT I LIKE IT)
THE ROLLING STONES
1974

Penned by Mick Jagger as a lighthearted riposte to the music journalists criticizing his artistic output, the cover of the 7-inch version of this track featured the Stone's trademark 'Tongue and Lip' motif. That logo was inspired by either the Hindu goddess Kali, or by Jagger himself, as owner of the world's largest lips and its longest tongue. Whoever's mouth and whatever the truth, it looks like it needs a drink. And what better, in this instance at least, than a Negroni Rock 'n' Roll? We know it's only gin, sweet vermouth and Campari, but we like it. Hell, what's not to like?

✻

MAKES 1

ice cubes

1 measure gin

1 measure sweet vermouth

1 measure Campari

orange wedges, to decorate

METHOD

Fill an old-fashioned glass with ice cubes. Add the remaining ingredients to the glass and stir. Decorate with orange wedges and serve.

Rebel Red Bull

REBEL REBEL
DAVID BOWIE
1974

The 'Rebel Rebel' lyrics reflect the dangers of mixing vodka with Red Bull and drinking it through a straw – you'll rip your dress, smear your lipstick and quite possibly end up declaring your love for a hot tramp. This was Bowie's goodbye to the glam-rock genre he pioneered – a track that left the world wanting more. The Rebel Red Bull has a similar effect, delivering a massive hit that leaves you wanting more.

✵

MAKES 2

ice cubes

4 measures vodka

Red Bull, to top up

METHOD

Fill 2 highball glasses with ice cubes. Divide the vodka between them. Top up with Red Bull and serve with straws.

Tequila Queen

KILLER QUEEN
QUEEN
1974

Queen's breakthrough track was the tale of a high-class call girl. It's classic Queen: elaborate harmonies, Brian May fret spanking and the type of flamboyant showmanship we came to know and love from rock's finest frontman. Our take here? She's Tequila Queen, tequila and grenadine, crème de cacao with single cream, guaranteed to blow your mind. Anytime!

*

MAKES 2

powdered drinking chocolate

1½ measures tequila

1½ measures white crème de cacao

175 ml (6 fl oz) single cream

4 teaspoons grenadine

ice cubes

METHOD

Dampen the rim of 2 chilled martini glasses and dip them into the drinking chocolate. Pour the tequila, crème de cacao, cream and grenadine into a cocktail shaker and add 8–10 ice cubes. Shake vigorously for 10 seconds, then strain into the chilled martini glasses.

Bohemian Daiquiri

BOHEMIAN RHAPSODY
QUEEN
1975

There isn't a cocktail in creation that could pay liquid tribute to 'Bohemian Rhapsody.' Over the course of that song's nearly six minutes, Queen conjured up a mock opera that pushed the technological limitations of the day to breaking point – and left listeners wondering WTF long before WTFs had been invented. To create a cocktail equivalent of 'Bo Rap' would be to stick every spirit ever created into a bucket, stir in some fruit, loads of mind-boggling LSD and then pray it somehow all comes together. Failing that, ladies and gentlemen, the Bohemian Daiquiri...

MAKES 1

ice cubes

2 measures light rum

1 measure sugar syrup

1 measure lime juice

lime wheel, to decorate

METHOD

Put all the ingredients into a cocktail shaker. Shake and strain into a martini glass. Decorate with a lime wheel and serve.

Born to Rum

BORN TO RUN
BRUCE SPRINGSTEEN
1975

An anthemic tale of escaping the constraints of small-town America (in this case Freehold, Noo Joysey), 'Born To Run' saw The Boss driving off into the distance in his hot-rod, accompanied by a young lady named Wendy. Not the most rock 'n' roll of names, but a man named Bruce could hardly complain. The track quickly became a call to disaffected post-adolescents everywhere, and years later it inspired this cocktail, the Born to Rum. Essentially, you're looking at a souped-up rum and cola. And you can forget about running or driving anywhere after one of these.

MAKES 2

ice cubes

4 measures golden rum, such as Havana Club 3-year-old

juice of 1 lime

cola, to top up

lime wedges

METHOD

Fill 2 highball glasses with ice cubes. Pour half the rum and lime juice into each and stir. Top up with cola, decorate with lime wedges and serve with straws.

Another Brick in the Wallbanger

ANOTHER BRICK IN THE WALL
PINK FLOYD
1976

The adorable kiddie chorus on 'Another Brick in the Wall' sang that they had no need for education – but how wrong they were. We never stop learning in life, kids, be it physics, grammar or how to mix up cocktails based on classic rock tracks. This one's a mix of vodka, Galliano and fresh orange juice, with ice and a slice. It's better known as a Harvey Wallbanger, a fact we know only because we have a raging thirst for knowledge. Not to mention a raging thirst for Another Brick in the Wallbanger. Get pouring.

✳

MAKES 1

6 ice cubes

1 measure vodka

3 measures fresh orange juice

1–2 teaspoons Galliano

orange wedge, to decorate

maraschino cherry, to decorate

METHOD

Put half the ice cubes into a cocktail shaker and the remainder into a highball glass. Add the vodka and orange juice to the shaker and shake until a frost forms on the outside of the shaker. Strain over the ice in the glass. Float the Galliano on top. Decorate with an orange wedge and maraschino cherry and serve.

Aniseed in the UK

ANARCHY IN THE UK
SEX PISTOLS
1976

The Sex Pistols followed the Young Anarchist's Handbook to the letter; living fast, swearing on chat shows and burning out after just one album, *Never Mind the Bollocks...* Happily, it yielded 'Anarchy in the UK', a call to arms to angry young kids who didn't know what they were actually angry about. Were the Pistols a cocktail band? Probably not, yet they'd have surely guzzled this one, for it contains tequila and Sambuca and takes its influence from the classic Flat Liner. Cheers!

MAKES 2

¾ measure tequila gold

4 drops Tabasco sauce

¾ measure Sambuca

METHOD

Pour the tequila into a glass. Float the drops of Tabasco over the top, then add the Sambuca.

Sex, Drugs and Rock 'n' Roll on the Beach

SEX & DRUGS & ROCK & ROLL
IAN DURY AND THE BLOCKHEADS
1977

Of course we're not condoning the use of those drugs mentioned in the title, unless it's a prescription for an ailment or a fungus or some such. That would be fine. Nor should you really be fornicating on the beach – the sand will play havoc and you may be arrested for indecency. The rock 'n' roll bit, though, we fully endorse. And in honour of Ian Dury and his Blockheads, might we suggest this reworking of the classic Sex on the Beach. It mixes vodka and peach schnapps with so much fruit – real, proper, fruity fruit – why, it's practically a sports drink.

MAKES 2

ice cubes

2 measures vodka

2 measures peach schnapps

2 measures cranberry juice

2 measures orange juice

2 measures pineapple juice (optional)

lemon and lime wedges to decorate

METHOD

Put 8–10 ice cubes into a cocktail shaker and add the vodka, schnapps, cranberry juice, orange juice and pineapple juice (if used). Shake well. Put 3–4 ice cubes into 2 highball glasses, strain the cocktail over the ice and decorate with the lemon and lime wedges.

Pisco Your Own Way

GO YOUR OWN WAY

FLEETWOOD MAC

1977

The standout track from an album crammed full of them, 'Go Your Own Way' charted the very public and painful breakup of guitarist Lindsey Buckingham and lead singer Stevie Nicks. The Pisco Your Own Way, based on the classic Pisco Collins, is a cocktail that involves pisco brandy, mixed with sugar syrup, lemon juice, soda water and peach bitters. Dress it up with a wedge of lemon and suck up that sweet Schadenfreude!

✻

MAKES 1

ice cubes

1 measure pisco

2 teaspoons sugar syrup

2 teaspoons lemon juice

4 measures soda water

2 dashes peach bitters

lemon wedge, to decorate

METHOD

Fill a Collins glass with ice cubes. Add the remaining ingredients and stir. Decorate with a lemon wedge and serve.

I Fought the Straw

I FOUGHT THE LAW
THE CLASH
1977

Originally written by Sonny Curtis of The Crickets, 'I Fought The Law' found global fame when punked up by The Clash. Here, we don't suggest you actually fight the law in any way, because crime never pays. But we do expect you'll be fighting every rational thought in your head that screams not to drink booze from a hollowed-out pineapple – especially through a straw! This reaction is entirely normal, but also wrong. Stick a straw in it and just keep telling yourself that you're drinking the very essence of rock 'n' roll excess. Although if that's true, why can't you stop humming 'Club Tropicana'?

✳

SERVES 2

1 pineapple

4 measures amber rum

1 measure Galliano

1 measure coconut cream

4 measures passion-fruit juice

1 banana

1 cup ice

orange wheels, to decorate

METHOD

Cut the top off the pineapple and use a pineapple corer to remove the flesh from inside the pineapple. Set aside the hollowed-out pineapple. Cut the pineapple flesh into chunks. Put 7 chunks of the pineapple and the remaining ingredients into a food processor or blender and blend until smooth. Pour into the hollowed-out pineapple, garnish with orange wheels and serve with umbrellas and straws.

You Took the Words Right Out of My Vermouth

YOU TOOK THE WORDS RIGHT OUT OF MY MOUTH

MEAT LOAF

1977

A natural-born showman with a taste for excess, Michael 'Meat Loaf' Aday might be a little disappointed by the cocktail we've created for him here. This, his debut single, was the type of big, brash, bombastic affair we grew to expect – a rock opera (a 'ropera', if you will) that divided opinion. The cocktail here is far more reserved, combining just Campari, sweet vermouth and prosecco. He requested we shove three umbrellas, five sparklers and a bat on top, but we settled on a single slice of orange. Because sometimes, Mr Loaf, less is more.

✻

MAKES 1

ice cubes

1 measure Campari

1 measure sweet vermouth

2 measures prosecco, chilled

orange wedge, to decorate

METHOD

Fill an old-fashioned glass with ice cubes. Add the Campari, sweet vermouth and prosecco and stir. Decorate with an orange wedge and serve.

Hey Ho! Pisco!

BLITZKRIEG BOP
RAMONES
1979

The Ramones' debut single was a furious assault on the senses, weighing in at just two minutes twelve seconds and featuring the legendary refrain of 'Hey, ho! Let's go!' Delivered over buzz-saw guitars by Joey Ramone's odd, plummy English accent, it was, claimed *Rolling Stone* magazine, the sound of a band throwing down the blueprint for punk rock. But more than that, it was the sound of a band throwing down the blueprint for the Hey Ho! Pisco! – a brandy-based concoction that takes its prompts from the classic Pisco Sour. Hey ho, let's go, then – directly to the drinks cabinet, and let's get mixing!

MAKES 2

ice cubes

4 measures pisco

2 measures lemon juice

4 teaspoons caster sugar

2 egg whites

2 dashes Angostura bitters

METHOD

Half-fill a cocktail shaker with ice cubes and fill 2 old-fashioned glasses with ice cubes. Add the pisco, lemon juice, sugar and egg whites to the shaker and shake until a frost forms on the outside of the shaker. Strain over the ice in the glasses, add half the bitters to each frothy head and serve.

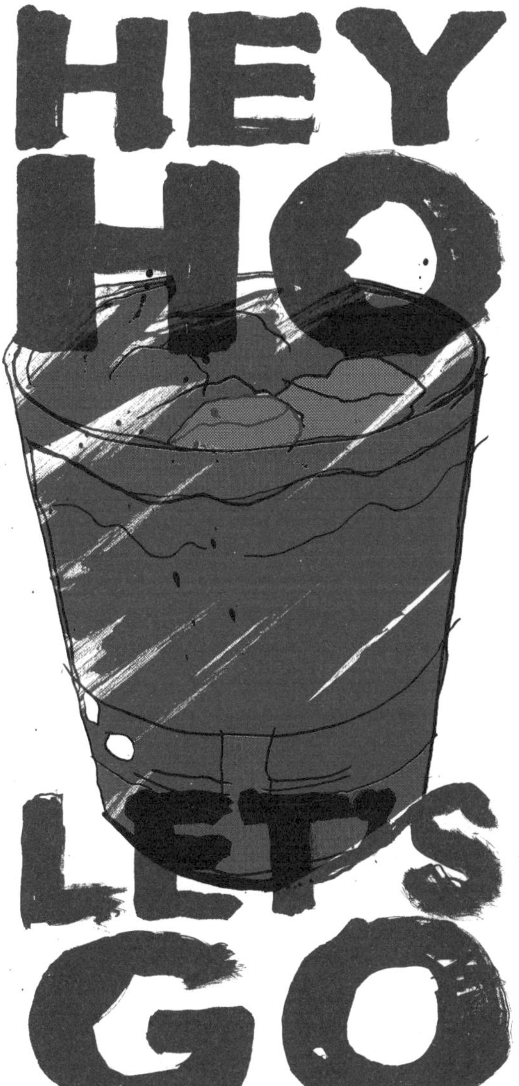
HEY
HO
LET'S
GO

Highball to Hell

HIGHWAY TO HELL
AC/DC
1979

Bigger and busier than Chris Rea's 'Road To Hell', AC/DC's 'Highway to Hell' dealt with the grinding nature of life on the road – the never-ending touring represented their own road to oblivion. Within months of its release, lead singer Bon Scott had died of acute alcohol poisoning. Now that could put a bit of a downer on your night if you think too much about it, so it's best not to dwell on it. Instead, mix up a Highball to Hell and turn up the music.

MAKES 2

4 measures brandy

2 measures Cointreau

250 ml (8 fl oz) bitter lemon

ice cubes

lemon slices, to decorate

METHOD

Pour the brandy, Cointreau and bitter lemon into a mixing glass and stir well. Put 8–12 ice cubes into 2 highball glasses and pour the mixture over the ice. Decorate with lemon slices and serve with straws.

Champagne in Vain

TRAIN IN VAIN
THE CLASH
1979

'Train in Vain' is that rarest of Clash tracks: a love song, about a train. Oddly though, the lyrics contain absolutely no reference to any train. Co-writer Mick Jones, knowing we'd be irked by the missing locomotive, explained that the rhythm of the track was like a train. It's still a great track, but come on: it's like suggesting you mix a Champagne cocktail and then leave the Champagne out. All you'd have then is a vodka and orange, and that wouldn't do. You deserve not to be mislead, people, so the Champagne goes into the Champagne in Vain and away we go. All aboard!

MAKES 2

2 lime wedges

2 measures lime vodka

2 measures orange juice

ice cubes

chilled Champagne, to top up

lime-rind twists, to decorate

METHOD

Squeeze the lime wedges into a cocktail shaker and add the vodka and orange juice with some ice cubes. Shake briefly and double-strain into 2 chilled Champagne flutes. Top up with chilled Champagne and decorate with lime-rind twists.

Southern Comfortably Numb

COMFORTABLY NUMB
PINK FLOYD
1979

Attempting to play bass and deliver lead vocals on a sold-out world tour can be a painful business. We know this because the lyrics for 'Comfortably Numb' concern Pink Floyd's Roger Waters, laid low with stomach cramps ahead of a show in 1977: he was warned that there would be no more aaaaaaaaah, but that he could end up feeling a little sick. He shuffled out on stage but could barely feel a thing. Of course, the Southern Comfortably Numb shares similarities. It too can numb the pain but it might make you sick. Hey, we all know the risks.

✻

MAKES 2

crushed ice cubes

4 measures Southern Comfort

2 measures lemon juice

1 measure maple syrup

chilled Champagne, to top up

lemon-rind strips, to decorate

METHOD

Put 8–10 crushed ice cubes into a cocktail shaker. Pour the Southern Comfort, lemon juice and maple syrup over the ice and shake until a frost forms on the outside of the shaker. Strain into 2 Champagne flutes and top up with chilled Champagne. Decorate with a lemon-rind strip and serve.

Appetite for Destruction

SHOTS & SHOOTERS

*

Welcome to the Interlude, dear drinker, a speakeasy kind of joint where things work a little differently. Now obviously we all agree that the rock 'n' roll cocktail is a creation worthy of great drunken celebration, but sometimes we need a change of pace. By which we mean: sometimes we just want to get drunk faster. Luckily, that's what shots and shooters were invented for.

Geography determines a shot from a shooter, but they're both designed for the same purpose: to get you tanked faster and in a more rock 'n' roll manner. Simply take one small glass of potent booze, knock it back in one (two at most), then slam it down on the counter and go again.

Shots and shooters are the 'Blitzkrieg Bop' of the booze world. Yes, there's a time and a place for 'Hotel California', but right now you want a short, sharp shock that makes you feel alive. And then another one that makes you feel even more alive. And then some more that make you feel 'free', 'happy', 'reckless', 'drunk', 'happy-drunk', 'drunken-drunk', 'mildly befuddled', 'ready to be sick on someone's shoes' and 'happy to pass out', in that order.

Now what we have here in the Interlude is six of the very best sharp shots and shooters known to mankind. From a Ring of Fireball to a Mandatory Kahlúa-cide, the names alone should serve notice of what lies in store.

So, if you think you can handle it, let's line 'em up.

Ring of Fireball

RING OF FIRE
JOHNNY CASH
1963

The 'Ring of Fire' is about the power of love and its ability to transform our lives, claimed Johnny Cash's daughter, Rosanne, so you can stop your sniggering now. Set to the sound of rousing mariachi-style horns, it became Cash's biggest-selling hit. A legendary hellraiser, a young Cash might have celebrated its success by rustling up the Ring of Fireball – a mean, rock 'n' roll mix of crazy absinthe, a dash of the digestif kümmel and a slug of the potent cinnamon schnapps Goldschläger. And it burns, burns, burns, the Ring of Fireball, the Ring of etc and so on.

MAKES 2

1 measure absinthe

1 measure ice-cold kümmel

1 measure Goldschläger

METHOD

Divide the absinthe into 2 shot glasses. Using the back of a bar spoon, slowly float half the kümmel over the absinthe in each glass to form a layer. Pour half the Goldshläger over the kümmel in the same way and serve.

Whole Shotta Love

WHOLE LOTTA LOVE
LED ZEPPELIN
1969

Tight-trousered rock god Robert Plant told listeners that he wasn't foolin', but you needed coolin', and then he proposed taking you back to schoolin'. By 'schoolin'', he really meant some good old-fashioned rock 'n' roll hanky panky. To be honest, Bob, we'd all probably prefer a nice cocktail. Particularly if it's the Whole Shotta Love – a punchy little concoction named in honour of Led Zep's finest hour (albeit not lyrically). Do note, however, that it contains ice cubes.

Because he was right. You do need coolin', baby.

✻

MAKES 2

ice cubes

1½ measures vodka

2 dashes Chambord

2 teaspoons pineapple purée

METHOD

Put some ice cubes into a cocktail shaker, add the vodka, Chambord and pineapple purée and shake briefly. Strain into 2 shot glasses and serve.

Sweet Home Alabama Slammer

SWEET HOME ALABAMA
LYNYRD SKYNYRD
1974

There once was a physical education teacher in Jackson, Florida, named Forby Skinner, but he preferred to go by his less-colourful middle name of Leonard. In his day job, Leonard Skinner taught various members of future southern rock royalty Lynyrd Skynyrd. In mocking tribute, they named their band after him, and the rest is now rock history. But had Lynyrd Skynyrd called themselves Fyrby Skynyrd instead, would they have found fame and fortune and written 'Sweet Home Alabama'? And if they hadn't done that, would we now have the Sweet Home Alabama Slammer? Who the hell knows? And in truth, who the hell cares? Let's drink!

MAKES 2

1 measure Amaretto di Saronno

1 measure Southern Comfort

1 measure sloe gin

METHOD

Divide the Amaretto di Saronno between 2 shot glasses. Do the same with the Southern Comfort and the sloe gin. Stir well.

Eye of the Jäger

EYE OF THE TIGER
SURVIVOR
1982

Commissioned to write the theme tune to *Rocky III*, US hair rockers Survivor originally wanted to call it 'Survival' but eventually settled on 'Eye of the Tiger'. An instant hit, it went on to become one of the biggest-selling songs of all time and would later inspire its very own cocktail. This cocktail, no less. And what a cocktail! Topping Jägermeister with a good slug of peppermint liqueur, it packs a punch that would drop Rocky to his knees. Serve with a plaintive cry of 'Adriannnnne!' But just don't try running up any steps afterwards.

MAKES 2

2 measures Jägermeister

2 measures peppermint liqueur

METHOD

Pour the Jägermeister into 2 shot glasses, then float half the peppermint liqueur over each.

Slippery Nipple When Wet

SLIPPERY WHEN WET
BON JOVI
1986

John Francis Bongiovi, Jr.'s Bon Jovi hit the big time with the release of this, the group's third album – yeah, that's right, the one with 'Livin' on a Prayer'. The album cover originally featured a buxom young lady in a wet T-shirt, suggesting Bon Jovi were not always the wholesome balladeers we know them as today. The cover got switched for something less chauvinistic but the suggestive title remained, and in its honour we present the Slippery Nipple When Wet. It's simply a shot of Sambora with half a measure of Bailey's floating on top. Hold up, no, Sambuca. Richie Sambuca. No, sorry, er...

MAKES 2

2 measures Sambuca

1 measure Bailey's Irish Cream

METHOD

Divide the Sambuca between 2 shot glasses, then do the same with the Bailey's floating it on top.

Mandatory Kahlúa-cide

MANDATORY SUICIDE
SLAYER
1997

We admit it: a thrash-metal track about inevitable death on the front line of war isn't the most obvious choice for a lighthearted cocktail tome. But as Slayer frontman Tom Araya has pointed out, the men and women who sign up for this 'mandatory suicide' do so to safeguard our freedom. And that's a freedom that includes flouncing around drinking lurid cocktails while making 'devil horn' hand gestures. The Mandatory Kahlúa-cide is based on a classic B-52. Reassuringly, it won't kill you, nor is it mandatory. That's freedom, alright.

*

MAKES 2

1 measure Kahlúa coffee liqueur

1 measure Bailey's Irish Cream

1 measure Grand Marnier

METHOD

Divide the Kahlúa into 2 shot glasses. Using the back of a bar spoon, slowly float half the Bailey's over each glass of Kahlúa. Pour the Grand Marnier over the Bailey's in the same way.

SideB

The Kids
Are Alright

THE MODERN AGE

✻

If this book were a record, or what our older readers might call a long-player, then you could expect its second half to be padded out with filler and fluff. Ah yes, that classic album tactic of shoving all the best tunes on Side A and all the tuneless tat on the flip. Rest assured, you won't find that happening here, readers. If anything, Side B might even rock harder than Side A – for this is all killer and absolutely no filler.

We're calling this 'The Modern Age'; a period stretching from 1980 to the present day that introduced us to some of the most influential figures in rock history – from Michael Stipe and Steven Morrissey to W. Axl Rose and Kurt Cobain, to namecheck but a few. Over the next 48 pages and 32 tracks, you'll encounter them all, plus the Satanists, the blood-crazed killers and the PE teacher who changed the course of rock history forever. You'll discover what Teen Spirit actually smells of and find out why 'another thing coming' is grammatically incorrect. Hell, you'll also finally learn the identity of the 34th greatest Western song ever written – and not before time.

All of this and more await you, accompanied of course by a classic rock 'n' roll cocktail on every page – because rocking hard can be thirsty work.

So, without further ado, let's put the needle to the groove and take it from the top...

Back in Black Russian

BACK IN BLACK
AC/DC
1980

A hard-rock masterpiece celebrating the life of former DC frontman Bon Scott, 'Back in Black' was penned by his replacement, Brian Johnson. Lyrically, it's a hotchpotch of nonsense that almost rhymes, but musically, it blows the doors off, being built on one of rock's greatest riffs. The Back in Black Russian cannot compete in terms of riffage, but it is at least black. Really black, on account of the Kahlúa. It's like, how much more black could it be?

MAKES 1

cracked ice cubes

2 measures vodka

1 measure Kahlúa Coffee Liqueur

METHOD

Put the cracked ice into an old-fashioned glass. Pour over the vodka and Kahlúa and stir.

Should I Stay or Mojito

SHOULD I STAY OR SHOULD I GO

THE CLASH

1982

If the name of this cocktail is a genuine question, the answer isn't an either/or. You should obviously stay and you should definitely mojito. Released in 1982, the song supposedly hinted at The Clash's impending implosion, and soon after its release the original four were no more. Ironically, drinking a Should I Stay or Mojito is likely to make you stay and talk to anyone about anything. Maybe The Clash should have tried it...

✳

MAKES 2

16 mint leaves, plus sprigs to decorate

1 lime, cut into wedges

4 teaspoons cane sugar

crushed ice

5 measures white rum

soda water, to top up

METHOD

Divide and muddle the mint leaves, lime and sugar in the bottom of 2 highball glasses and fill with crushed ice. Add half the rum to each, stir and top up with soda water. Decorate with mint sprigs and serve.

Rum to the Hills

RUN TO THE HILLS
IRON MAIDEN
1982

We're not going to pretend that 'Run to the Hills' is an obvious choice for a cocktail soirée. Yet despite the sobering subject matter, all most casual listeners will notice is that it has a really catchy chorus. Bruce Dickinson wails at us to run for our lives, and despite the threat of imminent death, we wail along too. And here's the clever parallel: taken neat, the Bacardi in our Rum to the Hills is way too heavy for most tastes. But add in a chorus of lemon juice and redcurrants and it suddenly packs a fabulously fruity kick.

MAKES 2

handful of redcurrants, plus extra
to decorate

1 measure sloe gin

4 measures Bacardi 8-year-old rum

1 measure lemon juice

1 measure vanilla syrup

ice cubes

METHOD

Muddle the redcurrants and sloe gin together in a cocktail shaker. Add the rum, lemon juice, vanilla syrup and some ice cubes. Shake and double-strain into 2 chilled martini glasses, decorate with redcurrants and serve.

The Number of Cassis

THE NUMBER OF THE BEAST
IRON MAIDEN
1982

Iron Maiden were accused of being devil worshippers upon the release of 'The Number of the Beast' in 1982, possibly on account of the lyrics screaming about the number 666. They were no such thing, of course, but as a nod to such horrors we've opted for a red cocktail to mimic the blood of a sacrificial child. In reality, it's nothing more sinister than crème de cassis, crème de framboise, cranberry juice, rosé wine and soda water, but nobody else needs to know that.

✽

MAKES 1

ice cubes

2 teaspoons crème de cassis

2 teaspoons crème de framboise

1 measure cranberry juice

3 measures rosé wine

3 measures soda water

raspberries, to decorate

METHOD

Fill a wine glass with ice cubes. Add the remaining ingredients and stir. Decorate with a couple of raspberries and serve.

You've Got Another Gin Comin'

YOU'VE GOT ANOTHER THING COMIN'
JUDAS PRIEST
1982

Judas Priest's early Eighties breakthrough was an eight-minute paean to grabbing life's chances. It went down as one of the defining moments in metal history and inspired this very cocktail, yet its lyrics were, in fact, grammatically incorrect. Respected linguists have pointed out that the phrase was originally another 'think' coming. Priest were clearly breaking the law – albeit the law of grammar. How very rock 'n' roll.

✳

MAKES 1 JUG

ice cubes

4 measures gin

6 measures Earl Grey tea

6 measures pink grapefruit juice

6 measures soda water

1 measure sugar syrup

maraschino cherries, to decorate

METHOD

Fill a jug with ice cubes. Add all the remaining ingredients and stir. Decorate with maraschino cherries and serve.

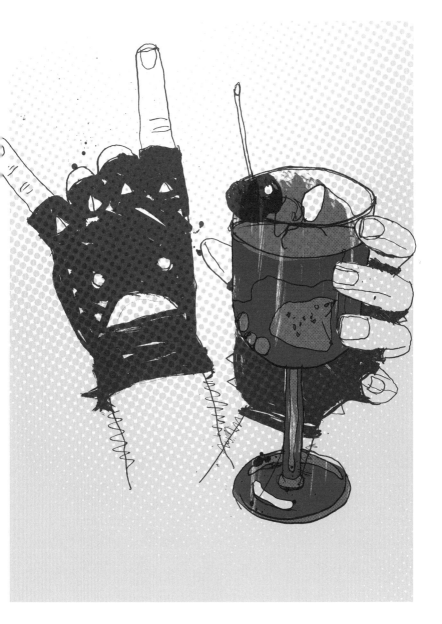

This Charming Manhattan

THIS CHARMING MAN
THE SMITHS
1984

Despite looking like a man who'd consume nothing more corrupting than the occasional Earl Grey, legend has it – corroborated by an admiring Noel Gallagher – that former Smiths frontman and founder Steven 'Morrissey' Morrissey does in fact sometimes drink booze. (Ironically, Johnny Marr is the teetotal one. Go figure.) So, in tribute to one of The Smiths' greatest singles, might we suggest The Charming Manhattan – a mix of bourbon, vermouth and Angostura bitters, topped off with a decorative cherry. You've got to think Morrissey would approve – especially if you garnish it with gladioli instead.

✳

MAKES 1

ice cubes

2 measures rye whiskey or bourbon

1 measure extra-dry vermouth

4 dashes Angostura bitters

fresh cherry, to decorate

METHOD

Put some ice cubes into a mixing glass. Add all the remaining ingredients and stir. Strain into a chilled martini glass. Decorate with a cherry and serve.

Sweet Child O'Brine

SWEET CHILD O' MINE
GUNS N' ROSES
1987

During the recording of their glorious debut album *Appetite for Destruction*, from which 'Sweet Child O' Mine' was taken, GN'R kept their creative juices topped up by drinking Night Train Express. An infamous brand of cheap, potent Californian wine, it was immortalized on track three, 'Nightrain'. In tribute, you could skull some cheap fortified wine and pass out in a gutter. Or you could mix up the more sophisticated Sweet Child O'Brine instead. It gets its name from the black olives and its kick from the vermouth and tequila – and it goes all the way up to 11.

✻

MAKES 2

ice cubes

4 teaspoons Noilly Prat

4 measures tequila gold (preferably añejo)

4 teaspoons brine from a jar of black olives

4 black olives, to decorate

METHOD

Fill a mixing glass with ice cubes and add the Noilly Prat. Stir to coat the ice thoroughly, then pour away the excess vermouth. Add the tequila and brine and stir until thoroughly chilled. Strain into 2 chilled martini glasses, decorate with black olives and serve.

With or Without Julep

WITH OR WITHOUT YOU

U2

1987

In U2's first US number-one single, Paul 'Bono' Hewson's lyrics were reputedly inspired by his struggles to reconcile his responsibilities as a married man with those as the lead singer of a globe-straddling rock band. It was getting him down. To understand quite how down, can you imagine someone had poured you a tall glass of Virginia Mint Julep, then asked you to leave before you could savour its sugary splendour? That's kind of the frustration Bono was feeling. So if With or Without Julep is a question, answer in the affirmative every time.

MAKES 2

18 mint sprigs, plus extra to decorate

2 teaspoons sugar syrup

crushed ice

6 measures bourbon

METHOD

Muddle half the mint and sugar syrup in the bottom of each glass (or, traditionally, iced silver mugs). Fill the glasses with crushed ice. Pour half the bourbon over the ice in each glass and stir gently. Pack in more crushed ice and stir until a frost forms on the outside of the glasses. Wrap each glass in a table napkin and serve decorated with mint sprigs.

Kir Comes Your Man

HERE COMES YOUR MAN
PIXIES
1989

And Your Man is, we trust, armed with a large, silver tray of Kir Royale, the classic French apéritif from which we take our inspiration here. Pixies frontman Black Francis wrote 'Here Comes Your Man' in his teens but considered it a little too 'pop' for his outsider sensibilities. Some might argue the mix of crème de cassis and Champagne in the Kir Royale may also be a touch too sweet for some tastes, but not us. Interestingly, 'Here Comes Your Man' was taken from the album *Doolittle*, and doing little may be a wise plan the day after a night on these.

✳

MAKES 1

1 measure crème de cassis

5 measures chilled Champagne

lemon twist, to decorate

METHOD

Add the crème de cassis and Champagne to a flute glass and mix. Expel the oils from a lemon twist into the glass by twisting the rind over the cocktail, then drape the lemon twist over the edge of the glass and serve.

Smells Like Martini Spirit

SMELLS LIKE TEEN SPIRIT
NIRVANA
1991

How does Teen Spirit smell, you're still wondering, all these years later? Well, it smells like sweet strawberries, like baby powder and like 'Pink Crush', whatever the hell that might be. That's because Teen Spirit was an American brand of girls' deodorant, as worn by a girlfriend of Kurt Cobain's in the early nineties. Its whiff inspired Nirvana's most famous track. And how does Martini Spirit smell? Mainly like gin, because it is mainly gin, mixed with a dash of dry vermouth. It won't make you smell like flowers or fruit, but it will inevitably have you screaming about an albino mosquito as you flail about the place after a few rounds.

✻

MAKES 2

ice cubes

1 measure dry vermouth

6 measures gin

stuffed green olives, to decorate

METHOD

Put 10–12 ice cubes into a mixing glass. Pour over the vermouth and gin and stir (never shake) vigorously and evenly without splashing. Strain into 2 chilled martini glasses, decorate each with a green olive and serve.

Rum As You Are

COME AS YOU ARE
NIRVANA
1991

'Come As You Are' was about the way that society expects people to behave, claimed reluctant grunge poster-boy Kurt Cobain. Although lyrically, it sounds like a cry for help, he wanted to spread a notion of nonconformity and we're happy to endorse that here. So while we suggest you mix up a Rum As You Are, it really is just a suggestion. If you want to make a Gin Genie or a Highball to Hell instead, knock yourself out.

✳

MAKES 2

ice cubes

2 dashes Angostura bitters

2 dashes lime bitters

2 teaspoons caster sugar

1 measure water

4 measures white rum

1 measure dark rum

lime-rind twists, to decorate

METHOD

Stir 1 ice cube with a dash of both bitters, 1 teaspoon sugar and half the water in each old-fashioned glass until the sugar has dissolved. Add the white rum, stir and add the remaining ice cubes. Add the dark rum and stir again. Decorate each glass with a lime-rind twist and serve.

Take the Sazerac

TAKE THE POWER BACK
RAGE AGAINST THE MACHINE
1991

In line with the overarching subject of their eponymous debut album, RATM's 'Take the Power Back' concerned itself with the band's leftist politics, the injustices of capitalism and the anti-imperialist struggles of the downtrodden, delivered via the medium of metal-crossed-rap and embellished with language you wouldn't play your grandmother. It was, in other words, some pretty heavy shit and it left your brain feeling beaten and bruised by the end of side two. Similarities can be drawn with our Take the Sazerac, a muscular mix of vodka and Pernod that can leave you feeling shaken and stirred.

*

MAKES 2

2 sugar cubes

4 drops Angostura bitters

5 drops Pernod

ice cubes

4 measures vodka

lemonade, to top up

METHOD

Put a sugar cube in 2 old-fashioned glasses and shake 2 drops of bitters over each. Add half the Pernod and swirl it around to coat the inside of each glass. Drop in 3–4 ice cubes and pour in half the vodka to each glass. Top up with lemonade, stir gently to mix and serve.

Jägerbombtrack

BOMBTRACK

RAGE AGAINST THE MACHINE

1991

Back in 1991, Rage Against The Machine released its eponymously-titled debut album, a vitriolic, pioneering rock-rap critique of America's social inequality. It was incendiary stuff, quite literally. Zack de la Rocha raged on the opener, 'Bombtrack', setting his sights on the politicians in power and never letting up. Happily, the Jägerbombtrack is far less angry and much less dangerous: simply drop a shot of Jäger into a tall glass of Red Bull and suck it back.

*

MAKES 1

6 measures energy drink, such as Red Bull

1 measure Jägermeister

METHOD

Pour the energy drink into a highball glass. Pour the Jägermeister into a shot glass. Carefully drop the shot glass into the highball glass containing the Red Bull so that it sinks to the bottom, and serve.

Eggnoggin' on Heaven's Door

KNOCKING ON HEAVEN'S DOOR

GUNS N' ROSES

1991

Bob Dylan's original was the definitive version of a song covered by numerous poppier artistes down the years (we're looking at you, Avril Lavigne). It was also chosen by *American Cowboy* magazine as the 34th greatest Western song ever written. So why have we replaced it here with the GN'R version? Because Axl Rose's caterwauling packs more of a kick than old Bob's folksy drawl, and that kick complements our Eggnoggin's potent mix of bourbon and dark rum far better. Drink while pondering this: if this was only 34th, what was the definitive Western song? Top marks and a top up for anyone who answers 'Ghost Riders in the Sky' by Stan Jones.

MAKES 4

2 eggs

3 tbsp granulated sugar

6 measures whole milk

8 measures double cream

2 measures bourbon

4 measures dark rum

ground nutmeg, to decorate

METHOD

Separate the eggs. Put the yolks into a large bowl and beat until pale, then gradually beat in the sugar until it is completely dissolved. Stir in the milk, cream, bourbon and rum. Put the egg whites in a clean bowl and beat until they form stiff peaks. Carefully fold the egg whites into the eggnog. Pour the eggnog into 4 old-fashioned glasses and sprinkle each with some ground nutmeg.

The Screwdriver Sleeps Tonite

THE SIDEWINDER SLEEPS TONITE

R.E.M.

1992

The prevailing mood of R.E.M.'s *Automatic for the People* album was one of gloom, dealing as it did with themes of death, suicide and the irreversible passage of time. Of course, that isn't to say it wasn't a great album, just that it was ill-suited to soundtrack a cocktail gathering. Apart, that is, from 'The Sidewinder Sleeps Tonite', the album's only ray of pop sunshine. Remixed here as The Screwdriver Sleeps Tonite, the blend of vodka with the sunny delight of the OJ should stave off any thoughts of mortality, suicide or the utter futility of it all. Cheers!

MAKES 1

2–3 ice cubes

1½ measures vodka

fresh orange juice, to top up

METHOD

Put the ice cubes into a highball glass. Pour over the vodka, top up with orange juice and stir lightly, then serve.

Red Right Brandy

RED RIGHT HAND
NICK CAVE & THE BAD SEEDS
1994

Said to have been inspired by a line in John Milton's epic poem *Paradise Lost*, the red right hand of Nick Cave's most dramatic murder ballad is said to refer to the vengeful hand of god. The owner of this red right hand is, we discover, a tall, handsome man carrying stacks of green paper. If you ever encounter this chap and he offers to buy you a drink, ask him for a Red Right Brandy – apple brandy, grenadine and a twist of lemon. He'll appreciate the clever wordplay, but he'll still murder you afterwards. Still, what a rock 'n' roll way to die!

MAKES 1

ice cubes

2 measures apple brandy

3 teaspoons grenadine

4 teaspoons lemon juice

METHOD

Add all the ingredients to a cocktail shaker. Shake, strain into a glass and serve.

Cognac Hole Sun

BLACK HOLE SUN
SOUNDGARDEN
1994

Soundgarden's finest hour – well, the group's most commercially lucrative track – is not what it might initially seem. Scratch the surface of the jangly guitars and that pretty melody and you'll uncover a metaphor for misery, suffering and quite possibly even the apocalypse. Similarly, sort of, the Cognac Hole Sun may initially appear sweet, as the lemon juice and maraschino cherries dance merrily upon your palate, but then the hard spirits hit home and you realize you're dealing with a fairly serious drink. If the apocalypse is to follow, pour yourself a large one and drink till the lights go out.

❋

MAKES 2

ice cubes

1 measure dry gin

1 measure apricot brandy

1 measure Cointreau

½ measure Galliano

½ measure lemon juice

maraschino cherries, to decorate

METHOD

Put some ice cubes into a cocktail shaker. Pour the gin, apricot brandy, Cointreau, Galliano and lemon juice over the ice. Shake, then strain into 2 large chilled martini glasses. Decorate each with a cherry.

Melon Daiquiri and the Infinite Sadness

MELLON COLLIE AND THE INFINITE SADNESS

THE SMASHING PUMPKINS

1995

Like the album of (almost) the same name, the Melon Daiquiri and the Infinite Sadness is a bittersweet affair – mixing a hefty slug of white rum with Midori, lime juice, sugar syrup, ice cubes and a melon wedge to garnish. It's also very strong from start to finish, which is more than can be said for the Pumpkins' beautiful but bloated album.

✻

MAKES 1

2 measures white rum

1 measure lime juice

1 measure sugar syrup

½ measure Midori

crushed ice

melon wedge, to decorate

METHOD

Shake the rum, lime juice, sugar syrup and Midori with plenty of crushed ice, then strain into a chilled martini glass. Decorate with a small wedge of melon

Julep with Butterfly Wings

BULLET WITH BUTTERFLY WINGS
THE SMASHING PUMPKINS
1995

With an opening line claiming that the world itself is a blood-sucking vampire, snarling, bald-headed, leather-skirt-wearing Pumpkin chief Billy Corgan set the tone and tempo for what follows in 'Bullet With Butterfly Wings'. It's a song about how angst became commodified, set to the sound of buzzing guitars and pounding drums, claimed Corgan and *Rolling Stone* magazine. Phew. Heavy stuff. By contrast, the Julep with Butterfly Wings is a refreshing glass of bourbon mixed with Angostura bitters and garnished with a sprig of mint – originally known as a Mint Julep. The two really shouldn't get on, but somehow they do.

✻

MAKES 2

18 mint sprigs, plus extra to decorate

2 teaspoons sugar syrup

4 measures bourbon

8 dashes Angostura bitters

METHOD

Muddle half the mint and sugar syrup in the bottom of each glass. Fill the glasses with crushed ice. Divide the bourbon and Angostura bitters over the ice and stir gently. Pack in more crushed ice and stir until a frost forms on the outside of the glasses. Serve decorated with a mint sprig.

Everlong Island Iced Tea

EVERLONG
FOO FIGHTERS
1997

Foos frontman Dave Grohl once explained that 'Everlong' was about a girl he'd fallen for, and was an attempt at encapsulating the sublime feeling of an overwhelming physical and spiritual connection to another person – culminating in perfect harmony when you sing together. There are definite parallels at play with the Everlong Island Iced Tea. Mix up a round of these and you'll soon feel a more physical and spiritual connection to your fellow boozers. But you'll also begin to think you can harmonize perfectly too. All evidence suggests otherwise, but hell, just go with it.

✳

MAKES 2

1 measure vodka

1 measure gin

1 measure white rum

1 measure tequila

1 measure Cointreau

1 measure lemon juice

ice cubes

cola, to top up

lemon wedges, to decorate

METHOD

Put the vodka, gin, rum, tequila, Cointreau and lemon juice in a cocktail shaker with some ice cubes and shake to mix. Strain into 2 highball glasses filled with ice cubes and top up with cola. Decorate with lemon wedges and serve.

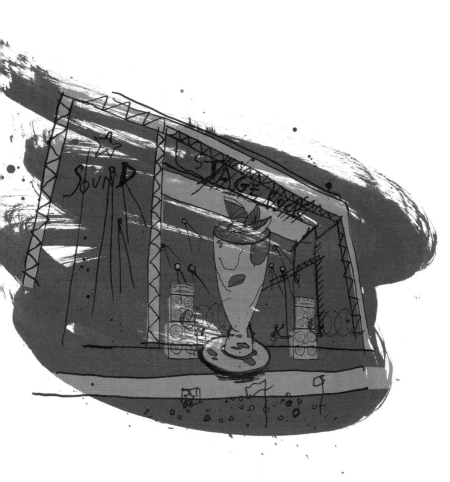

Don't Look Back in Sangria

DON'T LOOK BACK IN ANGER

OASIS

1995

During the peak of their creative powers in the mid Nineties. It's a common perception that Oasis were more often than not under the influence of strong booze. How else to explain them driving a Rolls Royce into a swimming pool or taking tea with Prime Minister Tony Blair? It's doubtful Sangria ever made their rider – the Spanish thirst-quencher hardly sat well with the whole 'Cool Britannia' vibe of the Nineties. Yet the fact that the word translates as 'bloodshed' in Spanish seems apt for the warring Gallagher brothers. Get on it, 'our kid' – and so on and so forth.

＊

MAKES 10–12

ice cubes

2 bottles light Spanish red wine, chilled

5 measures brandy

orange, lemon and apple wedges

cinnamon sticks

about 450 ml (16 fl oz) chilled lemonade, to top up

METHOD

Put some ice cubes into a very large jug. Add the wine, brandy, fruit wedges and one cinnamon stick and stir well. Top up with lemonade when you are ready to serve, and stir. Serve in wine glasses decorated with cinnamon sticks.

The Ghost of Tom Collins

THE GHOST OF TOM JOAD
BRUCE SPRINGSTEEN
1995

As you enjoy the sweet taste of this Tom Collins-inspired, gin-heavy classic, bear in mind it takes its lead from a Bruce Springsteen single inspired by Woody Guthrie's 'The Ballad of Tom Joad' and John Steinbeck's *The Grapes of Wrath*. The former sought to give voice to society's destitute, desperate and disenfranchised, the latter was set during the Great Depression and focused on drought, economic hardship, agricultural industry changes and, just, like, loads of other really gloomy stuff. Hey, come on, The Boss: stop harshing our buzz, man. Play us 'Born to Run' instead!

✳

MAKES 1

2 measures gin

1 measure sugar syrup

1 measure lemon juice

ice cubes

4 measures soda water

lemon wedge, to decorate

black cherry, to decorate

METHOD

Put the gin, sugar syrup and lemon juice into a cocktail shaker and fill with ice cubes. Shake to mix, then strain into a glass full of ice cubes and top up with the soda water. Decorate with a lemon wedge and a cherry and serve.

Angostura Bitter Sweet Symphony

BITTER SWEET SYMPHONY
THE VERVE
1997

'Bitter Sweet Symphony' was a bittersweet affair alright. A critically acclaimed hit on both sides of the Atlantic, The Verve were forced to hand over all their royalties following legal controversy over the use of a sample from the Rolling Stones' 1963 track 'The Last Time'. All lead singer Richard Ashcroft saw was $1,000 for writing the lyrics, and that's enough to turn a man to drink. So let's mix up the Angostura Bitter Sweet Symphony in sympathy. Based on a frisky mix of Angostura bitters, Grand Marnier and Champagne, it's bitter, but not as bitter as The Verve must be.

✻

MAKES 2

2 brown sugar cubes

6 drops Angostura bitters

2 measures Grand Marnier

chilled Champagne, to top up

orange twists, to decorate

METHOD

Put 1 sugar cube each into the bottom of 2 chilled Champagne flutes and add 3 drops of bitters to each. Add half the Grand Marnier to each glass and stir briefly. Top up with chilled Champagne, decorate each glass with an orange twist and serve.

OK Sambuca

OK COMPUTER
RADIOHEAD
1997

Truth be told, the five members of Radiohead wouldn't be on many people's guest lists for a cocktail party. There you are, mixing Sambuca and Kahlúa in a martini glass and feeling great about setting it on fire without burning down the house. Then you extinguish the flames by pouring over Bailey's Irish Cream and blue Curaçao and proudly announce the arrival of the OK Sambuca to your guests, and the room explodes in boozy applause. Only Radiohead wouldn't be applauding. They'd be far too busy banging on about airbags and consumerism to get with the good-time vibes in here tonight. Next time just put Andrew W.K. on the guestlist instead.

MAKES 2

2 measures Kahlúa Coffee Liqueur

2 measures Sambuca

2 measures Bailey's Irish Cream

2 measures blue Curaçao

METHOD

Divide the Kahlúa into 2 warmed martini glasses. Gently float half a measure of Sambuca over the back of a spoon into each glass so that it creates a layer on top. Pour the Bailey's and blue Curaçao into a shot glass. Pour the remaining Sambuca into a warmed wine glass and carefully set it alight, then pour it into the martini glasses. Pour half the Bailey's and Curaçao into each lit martini glass at the same time. Serve with straws.

Pretty Fly (For a Mai Tai)

PRETTY FLY (FOR A WHITE GUY)
THE OFFSPRING
1998

The white guy here being lampooned by The Offspring, for his 'bad-ass playa' act was fooling no-one. Far more Vanilla Ice than Ice Cube, he wore his cap backwards, his trousers round his backside and a big goldie-looking chain around his weedy-looking neck. The joke was on him, for he wasn't 'fly' in the slightest. And yet he did still inspire a classic rock cocktail, so who's laughing now?

✻

MAKES 2

ice cubes

crushed ice

2 measures golden rum

½ measure orange Curaçao

½ measure orgeat syrup

juice of 1 lime

2 teaspoons Wood's Navy Rum

2 maraschino cherries, to decorate

METHOD

Half-fill a cocktail shaker with ice cubes and put some crushed ice into 2 old-fashioned glasses. Add the golden rum, Curaçao, orgeat syrup and lime juice to the shaker and shake until a frost forms on the outside of the shaker. Strain over the ice in the glasses. Float half the Old Navy Rum on top of each glass. Decorate each with a maraschino cherry and serve.

Hate to Say Amaretto

HATE TO SAY I TOLD YOU SO
THE HIVES
2000

This Swedish five-piece were known for dressing like barmen – in white tuxedos, black shirts and black strides – and for penning this short, infectious blast of rock rebellion. It's admittedly a long shot, but if a Hive ever serves you a drink, order the Hate to Say Amaretto and tell him, with a primal scream, 'Because I WANNA!' He'd absolutely love that. He really would.

✻

MAKES 2

1 measure cherry liqueur

1 measure Amaretto di Saronno

1 measure bourbon

METHOD

Divide the cherry liqueur into 2 shot glasses. Using the back of a bar spoon, slowly float half the Amaretto di Saronno over each glass of cherry liqueur to form a separate layer. Layer the bourbon over the Amaretto in the same way and serve.

You Think I Ain't Worth a Dollar But I Feel Like a Whiskey and Pear

YOU THINK I AIN'T WORTH A DOLLAR BUT I FEEL LIKE A MILLIONAIRE
QUEENS OF THE STONE AGE

2002

As the man who once sang about nicotine, Valium, Vicodin, marijuana, ecstasy, alcohol and, of course, c-c-c-c-c-cocaine in 2000's Feel Good Hit of the Summer, it's probably fair to assume Queens frontman Joshua Homme is partial to the odd liquid 'straightener'. If we were pouring, we'd opt for this cocktail. It's our ode to the muscular opener from Queens' noisy and excellent *Songs for the Deaf*. It mixes bourbon, pear, redcurrant jam, lemon juice and sugar syrup, but absolutely no c-c-c-c-c-cocaine.

✳

MAKES 1

½ ripe pear cut into chunks, plus an extra slice, to decorate

———

3 teaspoons redcurrant jam

———

2 measures bourbon

———

4 teaspoons lemon juice

———

2 teaspoons sugar syrup

———

ice cubes

———

METHOD

Put the pear and jam into a cocktail shaker and muddle. Add the remaining ingredients and shake. Strain into a glass full of ice cubes, decorate with pear slices and serve.

———

White Russian of Blood to the Head

A RUSH OF BLOOD TO THE HEAD
COLDPLAY
2002

It's doubtful those young chaps in Coldplay take any kind of liquor, be it cocktails or otherwise. They seem too straight-laced for that and it would play havoc with their exam revision. But, if they were to mix a round up, they should try a White Russian of Blood to the Head, influenced by their 2002 album of a similar name. This little classic has its roots in the White Russian: equal parts vodka, Tia Maria and full-fat milk or double cream. Be warned, though, that drinking more than three of these will make you dance like Chris Martin. And no-one wants that.

MAKES 2

12 cracked ice cubes

2 measures vodka

2 measures Tia Maria

2 measures full-fat milk or double cream

METHOD

Put half the cracked ice into a cocktail shaker and divide the remaining cracked ice into 2 old-fashioned glasses. Add the vodka, Tia Maria and milk or cream to the shaker and shake until a frost forms on the outside of the shaker. Strain over the ice in the glasses and serve.

Mr Brightsidecar

MR BRIGHTSIDE
THE KILLERS
2004

The Killers introduced themselves to the world with this debut release, the tale of a man who knows his other half is doing the dirty on him. It was reputedly influenced by lead singer Brandon Flowers, the man whose other half was playing away. And yet, despite the gloomy subject, 'Mr Brightside' makes an almighty and euphoric racket. The Mr Brightsidecar takes its influence from the classic Sidecar and mixes good slugs of brandy and Cointreau or triple sec. Two or three of these and you too will be making an almighty and euphoric racket. Chin chin!

*

MAKES 2

3 measures brandy

1 measure Cointreau or triple sec

1 measure freshly squeezed lemon juice

lemon wedge, to decorate

METHOD

Shake the ingredients vigorously in a cocktail shaker with cracked ice. Strain into 2 chilled martini glasses and serve straight up with a lemon wedge.

Americano Idiot

AMERICAN IDIOT
GREEN DAY
2004

Short, sharp slice of post-punk, post-9/11 political posturing meets a long, tall flute of vodka and Champagne with a strawberry on the side. Now many readers will point out that drinking Champagne is not particularly punk rock, not even when it's mixed with vodka in this clever twist on the classic Americano. But this potent combination of grain and grape will get you tanked up double-quick, and that alone is pretty punk rock. Be warned, though, that being a Drunken Idiot of any nationality is a far bigger issue here. So respect the booze, people. Respect the booze.

MAKES 2

4 strawberries, plus extra to decorate

2 dashes sugar syrup

4 lime wedges

2 measures Absolut Kurant vodka

ice cubes

chilled Champagne, to top up

METHOD

Muddle the strawberries, sugar syrup and lime wedges in the bottom of a cocktail shaker. Add the vodka and some ice cubes. Shake and double-strain into 2 chilled Champagne flutes. Top up with chilled Champagne, decorate each glass with a strawberry and serve.

Keep the Advocaat Running

KEEP THE CAR RUNNING
ARCADE FIRE
2007

Despite being carried along on a wave of jaunty mandolin, 'Keep the Car Running' dealt with a sense of impending doom – lead vocalist Win Butler implores the driver to keep his car running so he can escape from the men who are coming to take him away. We have no such concerns, however, and we are imploring our host to keep the booze running. In this case, we're taking our inspiration from an Eldorado – so advocaat, white rum, white crème de cacao and a good slug of ice. Turn the engine off, driver. We may be here some time.

✳

MAKES 2

2 measures of white rum

2 measures of advocaat

2 measures of white crème de cacao

ice cubes

grated coconut, to decorate

METHOD

Put the white rum, advocaat and white crème de cacao in a shaker with plenty of ice. Shake well, then strain over ice into 2 chilled martini glasses. To serve, decorate with a sprinkling of grated coconut.

Use Some Toddy

USE SOMEBODY
KINGS OF LEON
2008

Along with 'Sex on Fire', 'Use Somebody' helped propel Kings from Deep South hipsters to stadium-filling superstardom almost overnight. Notoriously hard-livers, with hard livers to match, success hasn't much changed them – one suspects they'd still be happier drinking moonshine from a shoe than clinking Cristal. But we think they, and you, deserve something a little more sophisticated – like a Use Some Toddy. It's essentially an Irish Coffee, served in a hot toddy glass and, as the Kings themselves almost sang, you know that we could use some toddy.

✣

MAKES 2

2 teaspoons sugar

2 measures Irish whiskey

7 measures hot filter coffee, plus coffee granules to decorate, if liked

double cream, lightly whipped

METHOD

Warm 2 hot toddy glasses and add half the sugar and Irish whiskey to each one. Fill the glasses two-thirds full with hot filter coffee and stir until the sugar has dissolved. Float lightly whipped double cream over the top of each glass, pouring it over the back of a cold spoon. Decorate with coffee granules, if you like.

Index

Index

Discography

Discography

Notes on the recipes

The measure that has been used in the recipes is based on a bar jigger, which is 25 ml (1 fl oz). If preferred, a different volume can be used, providing the proportions are kept constant within a drink and suitable adjustments are made to spoon measurements, where they occur.

Standard level spoon measurements are used in all recipes.
1 tablespoon = one 15 ml spoon
1 teaspoon = one 5 ml spoon

The UK Department of Health and the U.S. Food and Drug Administration advise that eggs should not be consumed raw. This book contains some recipes made with raw eggs. It is prudent for vulnerable people such as pregnant and nursing mothers, invalids and the elderly to avoid these recipes.

This book includes recipes made with nuts and nut derivatives. It is advisable for those with known allergic reactions to nuts and nut derivatives to avoid these recipes.

It is also prudent to check the labels of pre-prepared ingredients for the possible inclusion of nut derivatives.

The UK Health Department recommends that men do not regularly exceed 3–4 units of alcohol a day and women 2–3 units a day, a unit being defined as 10 ml of pure alcohol, the equivalent of a single measure (25 ml) of spirits. Those who regularly drink more than this run an increasingly significant risk of illness and death from a number of conditions. In addition, women who are pregnant or trying to conceive should avoid drinking alcohol.

The U.S. Department of Health and Human Services recommends that men do not regularly exceed 2 drinks a day and women 1 drink a day, a drink being defined as 0.5 oz of pure alcohol, the equivalent of 1.5 oz of 80-proof distilled spirits. Those who regularly drink more than this run an increasingly significant risk of illness and death from a number of conditions. In addition, women who are pregnant or trying to conceive should avoid drinking alcohol.

An Hachette UK Company
www.hachette.co.uk

First published in Great Britain in 2016 by Mitchell Beazley, a division of
Octopus Publishing Group Ltd
Carmelite House
50 Victoria Embankment
London EC4Y 0DZ
www.octopusbooks.co.uk

Copyright © Octopus Publishing Group Limited 2016

Distributed in the US by
Hachette Book Group
1290 Avenue of the Americas
4th and 5th Floors
New York, NY 10020

Distributed in Canada by
Canadian Manda Group
664 Annette St.
Toronto, Ontario, Canada M6S 2C8

All rights reserved. No part of this work may be reproduced or utilized in any form
or by any means, electronic or mechanical, including photocopying, recording or by
any information storage and retrieval system, without the prior written permission of
the publisher.

ISBN 978-1-78472-136-7

A CIP catalogue record for this book is available from the British Library.

Printed and bound in China

10 9 8 7 6 5 4 3 2 1

Commissioning editor Joe Cottington
Editor Pauline Bache
Illustrator Ben Tallon
Additional text Nick Harper
Creative Director Jonathan Christie
Designer Jeremy Tilston
Production Controller Sarah Kramer